To:

From:

Published by Hallmark Gift Books,
a division of Hallmark Cards, Inc.,
Kansas City, MO 64141
Visit us on the Web at Hallmark.com.

Editorial development by Woohoo Ink, LLC, with
additional writing by Dan Taylor
All original text owned by and licensed from Woohoo Ink, LLC.

Editorial Director: Todd Hafer
Art Director: Kevin Swanson
Designer: Mark Voss
Production Artist: Dan C. Horton

ISBN: 978-1-59530-153-6
BOK3097
Printed and bound in China.

Introduction

I have always been fascinated by the power of humor to bring healing into nearly every area of our lives. After all, humor defuses conflict, enhances communication, combats isolation, and lowers guards. It lifts our spirits, broadens our perspectives, and helps us cope. It even reduces stress, decreases blood pressure, and strengthens the immune system. Best yet, humor has no calories and isn't taxable (yet), so there are very few downsides.

As a writer, I have received some of the most poignant, amazing letters from readers who have discovered humor's healing properties in the midst of life's most heart-breaking circumstances. I'll never forget the woman who wrote me two weeks after being diagnosed with breast cancer. She told me that, after reading a humorous piece I wrote on the therapeutic benefits of TV Land theme songs, she tried to quell her panic by asking her husband to sing the Gilligan's Island theme song with her. They went on to spend an hour singing the themes to Green Acres, The Brady Bunch, and more—until her anxious tears subsided and she was able to fall asleep.

Imagine that! In the hands of our creative, loving God, anything is possible. A donkey's jawbone becomes a weapon of mass destruction. A stable becomes a palace for a king. And a ditty about a man named Brady becomes a pathway to respite from pain.

Laughter really is good medicine.

In that spirit, I invite you to enjoy this book. The "Signs from God," as seen on billboards and in church parking lots and on bulletin boards nationwide. The bloopers from church bulletins. The clever quotes from the likes of Martha Bolton, Dan Taylor, Barbara Johnson, G.K. Chesterton, and even President Lyndon Baines Johnson. The stories, the jokes, and the Top-Ten lists.

The only bad thing I have to say about this book is based on the fact that I was sitting in a coffeehouse while reading some of the manuscript. And I can't say for sure, but I suspect that a snort-laugh ceases to be publicly acceptable when it causes a woman to spew latte from her nostrils.

Enjoy this book. Whether your life is characterized at the moment by major struggles or mundane stress, I encourage you to let these pages minister joy and healing to your spirit. Embrace the mirth. Ponder the insights. Laugh out loud.

Just don't drink while doing it.

By Karen Linamen, author of Just Hand Over the Chocolate and No One Gets Hurt

DAY
1

DON'T FORGET
TO CALL YOUR
MOTHER!

Top Ten Things To Do in Heaven
Besides Playing the Harp

10. Tune the harps.

9. Double-check the harp inventory.

8. Post on harpnut.com blog.

7. Make up hilarious puns like
   "Just harpy to be here!"

6. Fuss with robe.

5. Re-tune the harps.

4. Hide in harp case, jump out,
   and scare unsuspecting angels.

3. Call radio stations, shout "More harp!"
   and hang up.

2. Tell yourself that 3,459th chair out of seven
   billion in the harp section is not that bad.

1. Sketch designs for harp tattoos.

DAY
3

Signs from God

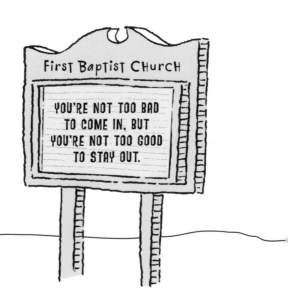

FIRST BAPTIST CHURCH

YOU'RE NOT TOO BAD
TO COME IN, BUT
YOU'RE NOT TOO GOOD
TO STAY OUT.

DAY
4

Q: We're having our first child soon—a boy.
We'd like to give him a biblical name.
We're thinking Matthew. Do you approve?

A: No, we're sorry, but we don't. Matthew is
indeed a good biblical name, but it's too common.
Every Tom, Dick, and Harry is named Matthew.

DAY 5

Seen on a Bumper Sticker

If you're looking for a sign from God
to go back to church, maybe this is it . . .

A Voice from Above

Two outdoorsmen from Texas went to Minnesota for a little ice fishing. After setting up a tent and sorting their equipment, they began to drill a hole in the ice. As they fired up their chainsaw, however, they heard a booming voice from above them: "There are no fish under that ice!"

Startled, the men looked at each other. "Is . . . is that you, Lord?" one of them asked.

The voice boomed again: "No, I'm the owner of this ice-skating rink, and I'm telling you guys for the last time – there are no fish under that ice!"

DAY
7

"Stressed out?
Don't give up—
Moses was once a basket case."

Chaplain Mark Sperling

DAY
8

Mom's Priceless Art Treasures

The Hand Print

The Portrait

The Clay Thing

REVILO

DAY
9

What's in a Number?

In some congregations, children ten and under get to attend Children's Church, while those eleven and up are expected to worship with the adults. In an attempt to buck the system, one mom of an eleven-year-old girl told her daughter, "Now remember, Anna, if anyone asks, you are only ten. Got it?

Anna nodded her head.

At the beginning of Children's Church, the leader approached Anna. "How old are you?" he asked.

"Ten, sir," she said.

"Ah, and when will you be eleven?"

The girl thought for a moment. "As soon as Children's Church is over."

DAY
10

Seen on a Bumper Sticker

Forbidden fruit creates many jams!

DAY
12

A Report from the Front

Because his wife had the flu, her husband attended a
Sunday service without her. When he returned home,
she asked for a recap.

Wife: "How was the service this morning?"

Husband: "Good."

Wife: "And the special music?"

Husband: "Good."

Wife: "Attendance is sometimes low this time of year;
how was the turnout?"

Husband: "Good."

Wife: "What was the sermon topic?"

Husband: "The importance of good communication."

DAY 13

A Riddle Overheard at a
National Pastoral Convention

Q: What do you need to make a small fortune
   in the ministry?

A: A large fortune.

Flower Power?

A young business executive visited his priest for some marital counseling. At the conclusion of their session, the priest advised the executive to apologize to his wife and give her a token of his remorse. "You know," the priest said, "say it with flowers."

"OK," the exec agreed. "I'll pick up a rose on the way home."

"Just one?" the priest said.

"Well, I'm a man of few words."

DAY
16

Signs from God

SILICON VALLEY BIBLE CHURCH

READ THE BIBLE.
IT'S USER-FRIENDLY,
AND WE OFFER TECH
SUPPORT EVERY SUNDAY
MORNING AT 11.

DAY
17

A Grave Matter

An elderly man decided it was time to visit his minister to discuss matters related to his funeral service. "The first question that comes to my mind," the minister said, "is whether you want to be buried or cremated . . ."

The old gentleman thought for a few minutes, then replied, "I really don't have a preference. Surprise me!"

DAY
18

Put 'Em Where It Hurts

A frustrated dad of a teenager was complaining to his church's youth pastor. "I try to discipline Scott by sending him to his room right after supper," he said, "but he has his own high-def TV, a killer sound system, a state-of-the-art computer, a private phone, and a mini-fridge. I should be so lucky."

"You know what you need to do?" the youth pastor advised.

"What?" the father said.

"Next time, send Scott to your room!"

DAY
19

Thou Shalt Have No Other Hitachis
Before Me . . .

Upon their return from an excursion to planet earth,
a team of Martian explorers presented their leader
with a high-definition flat-screen TV.
"We couldn't manage to bring you back any actual
earthlings," one explorer explained, "but we were able
to get our hands on one of their gods."

DAY
20

Signs from God

First Presbyterian Church

VISITORS WELCOME,
MEMBERS EXPECTED.

Noah and the 'Roos

While he waited for the great flood to begin, Noah had to house the various animals. He built a special eight-foot-high fenced enclosure for the two kangaroos, but during their first night in the fence, they escaped. Noah found them hopping around outside the following morning. So he increased the fence's height to 15 feet, but the kangaroos escaped again.

Exasperated, he added another 15 feet to the enclosure. The kangaroos still escaped. After Noah put the 'roos back inside the fence, they were approached by one of the giraffes. "How high do you think Noah will build the fence this time?" the giraffe asked.

"I don't know," answered the female kangaroo. "But he might eventually get it to 1,000 feet if he keeps leaving the gate unlocked."

Dinosaur Moms

Signs from God

DAY
24

A Modern Beatitude

Blessed are you when you have little stumbles,
for they prevent big falls.

DAY
25

Maybe the best place for "the buck" to stop is in the offering plate?

Signs from God

DAY 27

If you're green with envy,
you're ripe for trouble.

DAY
28

Signs from God

UNITED CHURCH of Christ

UNDER THE SAME
MANAGEMENT FOR
2,000-PLUS YEARS!

DAY
30

A Pastoral Proverb

"Receiving accolades from your congregation after a powerful sermon is like smoking a cigar; it won't hurt you if you don't inhale."

The Rev. Robert St. John

DAY 31

"Life is a spiritual journey, and, no, we're not 'there' yet."

Keely Chace

DAY
32

Signs from God

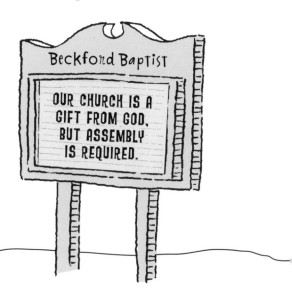

Beckford Baptist

OUR CHURCH IS A
GIFT FROM GOD,
BUT ASSEMBLY
IS REQUIRED.

DAY 33

God Is Love, and So Is Dog

In a Sunday school class, students were asked to write a short prayer. One six-year-old boy fidgeted in his chair, frowned thoughtfully, and nibbled on his pencil for several minutes before committing his prayer to paper. It read, "Dear God, please help me to be the person my dog thinks I am."

DAY
34

A Church Fashion Tip

It really doesn't matter how you dress for church,
as long as you don't get all wrapped up in yourself.
That is definitely not a good look for you!

DAY
35

Signs from God

Saint John's Catholic Church

NOW OPEN
BETWEEN EASTER
AND CHRISTMAS!

DAY 36

The **OPTIMIST** sees the glass as **half FULL.**

The **PESSIMIST** sees the glass as **half EMPTY.**

THE **MOTHER** sees the glass as **just one more thing to wash.**

DAY
38

Seen on the Door of a Church Nursery

"We will not all sleep, but we will all be changed . . ."

1 Corinthians 15:51

DAY
39

Signs from God

Harvest Christian Fellowship

ENJOY OUR
HAPPY HOUR,
SUNDAYS AT 11!

DAY
40

A Pastor's Proverb

"Some days you wake up thinking, Good morning,
Lord! On others, it's more like, Good Lord,
it's morning!"

Chaplain Mark Sperling

Signs from God

Grace Presbyterian Church

IF YOU THINK JOHN AND
PAUL WERE MEMBERS OF THE
BEATLES, MAYBE IT'S TIME
FOR YOU TO ATTEND HERE.

DAY
42

"If you want to know what God thinks of money,
just look at the people he gave it to."

Dorothy Parker

THINGS I'VE LEARNED:

A UNIVERSAL REMOTE CONTROL DOES NOT, IN FACT, ALLOW YOU TO CONTROL THE UNIVERSE.

$E = MC^2$

broce

DAY
44

Faith is the postage stamp
on our prayers.

DAY
46

"My soul has had enough chicken soup.
It wants chocolate!"

Cherie Rayburn

DAY
47

"Life is like a box of chocolates, which means skinny chicks can't really enjoy life, so HA!"

Tina Neidlein

DAY
48

Something to Ponder

What if God is asking us for a sign?

DAY 50

I was fooled by crab cakes once.

I will not be fooled again.

I mean, c'mon...

where's the frosting?

Possible Excuses to Use if You Get Caught
Sleeping in Church

1. "At the blood bank, they told me this might
   happen."
2. "Someone must have put decaf in the fellowship-
   area coffee pot this morning."
3. "I wasn't sleeping; I was just meditating on the
   sermon."
4. "...and bless my beloved fellow worshippers.
   In God's name, amen."

DAY
52

You've Been Warned

If you're at a congregational business meeting, and
someone says, "Well, to make a long story short . . . ,"
it's already too late.

DAY 53

"All I really need is love, but a little chocolate now and then doesn't hurt!"

Lucy Van Pelt

DAY
55

A Modern Beatitude

Blessed are the flexible, for they shall never be
bent out of shape.

DAY
56

A Definition from the Church Secretary

A memo from the pastor lies somewhere between
an official document and a perfectly good blank sheet
of paper.

DAY 57

If you're not
going to
SNORT,
why even laugh.

DAY
58

"Remember not only to say the right thing at the
right place, but to leave unsaid the wrong thing at
the tempting moment."

Benjamin Franklin

DAY
59

Signs from God

Grace Fellowship

WHOLE HEARTS WANTED.
BROKEN ONES WARMLY
ACCEPTED TOO.

DAY 60

Today a minister can send a whole sermon around the world in one-seventh of a second, but it might take him years to force one simple principle through a quarter-inch of human skull.

DAY
61

You've Been Warned

If you prove to be a talented church volunteer, you'll be "volunteered" for everything. But if you're really, really talented, you'll be able to get out of it.

DAY
62

Signs from God

JOHNSTOWN Family CHurch

TODAY'S SERMON:

SHOULD YOU TITHE FROM YOUR
NET OR GROSS INCOME?
(HINT: DO YOU WANT NET
BLESSINGS OR GROSS BLESSINGS?)

DAY
63

Signs from God

SLEEPLESS?
DON'T COUNT SHEEP;
TALK TO THE
SHEPHERD.

DAY
64

Can God inspire a sermon so boring that God
can't stay awake through it?

DAY
65

What's over your head
is under God's feet.

DAY
66

Signs from God

Signs from God

Culver Christian Church

IF YOU DON'T WANT TO DEAL WITH THE DEVIL, STAY OUT OF HIS SHOP.

DAY
68

A Pastor's Plea

"Please live a good life – I don't want to lie
at your funeral."

The Rev. Robert St. John

Top Ten Ways to Tell You're an "Old School" Christian

10. All the verses you've memorized are King James.

9. Most of those verses involve "smiting."

8. You know the fifth verse of every hymn with five verses.

7. You're angry/hurt whenever they skip the fifth verse.

6. You tithe on the gross, not the net.

5. On your calendar, every Sunday night and every Wednesday night is booked -- forever.

4. You approve of facial hair only when it's for a Passion Play.

3. You don't really approve of Passion Plays.

2. All of your children have names from the Bible.

1. You have five or more children.

DAY
70

Signs from God

PRAY, BUT ONLY
ON DAYS ENDING
IN "Y."

Ask the Theological Know-How Dudes

Q: I have been to several Christian stores but cannot find any decent manna. What gives?

A: Don't be discouraged; a good manna is hard to find.

DAY
73

If God is your copilot,
maybe it's time to switch seats.

DAY
74

Signs from God

DAY 75

"Beware the self-made man; he tends to worship his creator."

Drew Cody

DAY
76

Q: I'm deeply opposed to Earth Day; it seems pagan and New Age to me. Your thoughts?

A: We must respectfully disagree. We think it's a good idea to have a yearly holiday that reminds folks, especially our politicians, which planet we live on.

DAY
79

Seen on a Bumper Sticker

Stomach upset?
Try swallowing your pride.

DAY
81

"Be careful about letting it all hang out. You might not be able to get it tucked back in."

Robin St. John

DAY
82

Seen on a Bumper Sticker

Please don't drive faster than your
guardian angel can fly!

DAY
83

Something to Ponder

"Have you read the good book lately?
(There will be a test.)"

One thing seemed certain.
Squeaky would never be asked
to serve as the entertainment
chairman again.

You know it's time to join your church's
Seniors Group when . . .

1. You try to straighten out the wrinkles in your socks, then realize you aren't wearing socks.

2. Even when you stay home, your back goes out.

3. It takes you twice as long to look half as good for Sunday service.

4. Most of the names of your Facebook friends start with "Dr."

5. It takes you longer to rest up than it did to get tired.

6. The only birthday gift you want from your fellow parishioners is NOT to be reminded of your age.

7. At the breakfast table, you hear lots of Snap! Crackle! and Pop! But you aren't eating cereal.

8. You sit in a rocking chair, but you can't get it started.

9. Your idea of weight-lifting is standing up after a long sermon.

10. Your pastor regularly compliments you on your patience, but you know that you probably just weren't paying attention.

DAY
89

Noah was a brave man who set sail in a wooden boat that included at least two termites as passengers.

DAY
90

Q: I'm confused about the End Times. I don't know whether to be an amillennialist, premillenialist, or postmillennialist . . .

A: We recommend you adopt our position. We're panmillenialists. That is, we believe everything will pan out in the end.

DAY
91

Top Ten Reasons NOT to Sleep in
This Sunday

10. Mrs. Abernathy might wear that dress.
The one she wore two Easters ago.

9. Mrs. Abernathy might get into a fight with
someone. Like she did two Easters ago.

8. Leftover potluck desserts.

7. The unpredictable antics of live goats!
(Valid on Live Nativity Sunday only.)

6. The unpredictable antics of kids jacked up on
candy they won by memorizing verses during
Sunday School.

5. Two words: bulletin typos.

4. Every now and then, there's a cool Old Testament
story where people have spear fights and stuff.

3. You might finally get that parking space right by
the front door.

2. Football doesn't start till noon anyway.

1. When you sleep at church, you're never
sleeping alone.

DAY
93

LIVING LIKE
THERE IS NO GOD?
BETTER PRAY
YOU'RE RIGHT.

DAY 94

What a caterpillar calls the end of the world,
God calls a butterfly.

DAY
95

A Pastor's Proverb

"A Bible in the hand is worth two on the bookshelf."

The Rev. Robert St. John

Signs from God

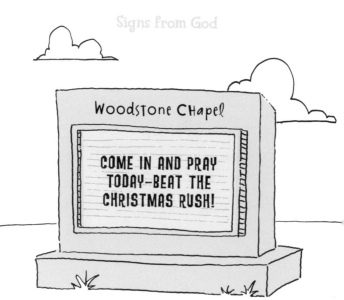

Woodstone Chapel

COME IN AND PRAY
TODAY—BEAT THE
CHRISTMAS RUSH!

Seen on a Bumper Sticker

HWJD?
(How would Jesus drive?)

DAY
98

Signs You Need Pastoral Counseling
for Your Coffee "Problem"

1. You refer to your fellow parishioners as your
   "coffee mates."

2. You gargle with coffee-flavored mouthwash.

3. You can be found in the church basement playing
   Ping Pong. Without an opponent.

4. You don't tan; you roast.

5. You can't wait to go to bed each night, just so you
   can "wake up and smell the coffee."

6. The main reason you have a job is for the
   coffee breaks.

7. To you, being called a "drip" is a compliment.

8. You named your cats Cream and Sugar.

9. You have lobbied to have Juan Valdez declared
   a saint.

10. Your face is on the Colombian postage stamp.

DAY
100

Signs from God

FELLOWSHIP BIBLE CHURCH

ASK US ABOUT
OUR FREE TRIP
TO HEAVEN!

DAY
101

Were there woodpeckers on Noah's ark?

DAY
102

Signs from God

DAY
103

"No one will ever win the battle of the sexes.
There's too much fraternizing with the enemy."

Henry Kissinger

DAY
104

Bulletin Bloopers

Barbara remains in the hospital and needs blood donors for more transfusions. She is also having trouble sleeping and requests tapes of Pastor Jack's sermons.

The rector will preach his farewell message tonight, after which the choir will sing "Break Forth into Joy!"

Next Thursday there will be tryouts for the choir. They need all the help they can get.

Remember the big all-church swap meet next Saturday in City Park. Husbands, bring your wives and get a great bargain!

DAY
105

On Prayer and Golf

"Prayer never seems to work for me on the golf course. I think this has something to do with my being a terrible putter."

The Rev. Billy Graham

OLD McDONALD HAS A COW

DAY
107

Seen on a Bumper Sticker (of a Hearse)

Don't wait for one of these
to take you to church.

DAY
108

"When I was young, the Dead Sea was alive."

George Burns

DAY
109

Wisdom for the Ages

Two heads are better than one, but you'll need twice the aspirin.

When the meat loaf explodes, it's done.

Let the chips fall where they may—but don't let the dip land on the carpet!

It's always darkest just before the dawn—especially if you're in bed with the covers over your head.

Rats desert a sinking ship—and immediately change travel agents.

Martha Bolton

DAY
110

Signs from God

Bayside Baptist Church

FIGHT TRUTH DECAY.

DAY
111

"Laughter is the shortest distance between two people."

Victor Borge

DAY
112

A Modern Proverb

"Sometimes one likes foolish people for their folly,
better than wise people for their wisdom."

Elizabeth Gaskell

DAY 114

A Few Thoughts on Aging

There are a few advantages to getting older.
For example, you can't nurse a grudge that you
can't remember.

A friend reminds me that it's not what you go
through in life that counts; it's how you look while
you're going through it.

Now that I have entered midlife, I have learned a new
rule: Never apply makeup during a hot flash, because
it will slide right off your face.

Anita Renfroe

DAY
115

"If at first you don't succeed, see if the loser gets a nice consolation prize."

Barbara Johnson

DAY
116

Hymn Confusion

A children's-church leader stopped her class one morning—right in the middle of a hymn they were singing.

"What words did you just sing?" she asked. "Something doesn't sound quite right."

A young girl, the group's loudest vocalist, shot her hand in the air. "We're singing, 'Oh, the constipated, cross-eyed bear!'"

The leader shook her head and went to the whiteboard, where she wrote the correct title of the song for her class: "Oh, the Consecrated Cross I Bear."

DAY
117

A Bit of Marriage Advice from
Mrs. Billy Graham

"In marriage, sometimes we submit; sometimes
we outwit."

Ruth Bell Graham

DAY
118

"Youth is a gift of nature, but age is a work of art."

Garson Kanin

DAY 121

Why Miracles Are Better
Than Miracle Drugs

Tired of pesky backache pain?
Get fast relief from Dolocaine!
(Warning: May cause inflammation, nausea, nosebleed,
constipation, swollen ankles, smelly feet, canker sores
and prickly heat, scaly skin and dysentery, typhoid fever,
beriberi, measles, mononucleosis, lockjaw, scurvy, halitosis,
memory loss, excessive sweating, plantar warts and
mattress wetting, ringworm, pinworm, migraine, strep,
a vague and vexing loss of pep, sunburn, asthma,
palpitations, really weird hallucinations, charley horses,
creaky knees, toxic shock and Lyme disease.)
The side effects are all quite rare, so ask your doctor—
if you dare!

DAY
122

"I have been trying to learn our church's new computer system, and this is what I've learned: Artificial intelligence is no match for 100-percent natural stupidity."

The Rev. Jerry Springston

DAY
123

Not Accurate, but True All the Same

A group of Sunday school students were being tested on their Bible memory verses. A six-year-old boy stood to recite John 3:15. "I know this one," he assured the teacher. "Whosoever believeth in Jesus shall have ever-laughing life!" The teacher gave him partial credit.

DAY
124

"This too shall pass. Now would be good."

Dee Ann Stewart

Major League Baseball's All-Church Team

Catcher: Steve Christmas
1st Base: Jim Gentile
2nd Base: Lave Cross
3rd Base: Max Bishop
Outfield: Bob Christian
Outfield: Howie Nunn
Outfield: Johnny Priest
Designated Hitter: Bris Lord
Pitchers: Bill Parsons, Preacher Roe,
and Adrian Devine

DAY
126

"Whoever said you only go around once in life never had Bible School carpool duty."

Dan Taylor

MY BOLOGNA
HAS A
MIDDLE NAME.

IT'S MARIE.

DAY
128

Bulletin Bloopers

Our associate pastor is proud to announce the new tithing campaign: "I Upped My Pledge. Up Yours!"

Reminder: Housing is needed for the visiting missions drama team next week. If you can put up with these performers for a day or two, please notify the pastor.

Hungry? Then come pot-licking with us in the Fellowship Hall after the service next Sunday!

Please remember to pray for Mrs. Johnson, who will be entering the hospital this week for a battery of testes.

DAY
130

"I'm beginning to question my church's commitment to nutrition. At our church potlucks, carrot cake counts as a vegetable."

The Rev. Mark Sperling

DAY
132

A Pastor's Proverb

"The laughter of the children in the congregation
is very comforting—unless it's directed at you."

The Rev. Jerry Springston

DAY
133

The Forgotten Beatitude

Blessed are you if you can laugh at yourself;
for you shall never cease to be amused.

DAY
136

Signs from God

FOR GOD SO LOVED
THE WORLD THAT
HE DID NOT SEND
A COMMITTEE.

DAY 137

Bulletin Bloopers

The peacemaking meeting originally scheduled for today has been canceled due to a conflict.

Ladies, don't forget the rummage sale. It's a chance to get rid of those things not worth keeping around the house. (Don't forget to bring your husbands!)

Our youth basketball team is back in action Friday night at 8 in the Rec Hall. Come out and watch us stomp Sacred Heart of Mary.

Don't forget next month's Prayer & Fasting conference. Registration is only $50, and that price includes all meals and snacks.

DAY
138

"Why is it that when we talk to God, we're praying,
but when God talks to us, we're schizophrenic?"

Lily Tomlin

DAY
139

Potluck Tip

Avoid any meat dish that bears tread marks.

DAY
140

A Theologian's Take on Golf

"Golf is an expensive way of playing marbles."

G.K. Chesterton

DAY
142

Bulletin Bloopers

The "Using Time Wisely" conference has been rescheduled to February 28–30.

Bertha Belch, a missionary from Africa, will be speaking tonight at Calvary Memorial Church in Racine. Come tonight and hear Bertha Belch all the way from Africa.

Our church will host a potluck dinner tonight, featuring live music. This promises to be a memorable evening for both the young and the young in heat.

The sermon this morning: "Jesus Walks on Water." The sermon for tonight: "Searching for Jesus."

DAY
143

"I'm not a vegetarian because I love God's animals;
I'm a vegetarian because I hate plants!"

Drew Cody

DAY
144

A Pastor's Proverb

"A great prayer partner keeps your secrets, laughs at your jokes, and always has the wisdom to know the difference."

The Rev. Robert St. John

DAY
145

Something to Ponder

If psychics are so brilliant, how come they need
caller I.D.?

DAY
146

"In the beginning, there was nothing. Then God said, 'Let there be light!' And there was light. There was still nothing, but you could see it a whole lot better."

Groucho Marx

DAY
147

Life is fragile.
Handle with prayer.

DAY
150

"Today's gas prices are higher than a dog's hopes at a church picnic!"

The Rev. Robert St. John

DAY
151

Potluck Tip

Rice cakes taste a whole lot better dipped in
hot fudge.

DAY
152

Signs from God

DOING NOTHING
IS HARD; HOW DO
YOU KNOW WHEN
YOU'RE FINISHED?

You Know It's Time to Clean When . . .

1. The flowers on your bedsheets start taking root.
2. You catch your kids tobogganing down the dirty-clothes pile.
3. You've written more than three phone messages in the dust on your dresser.
4. You can hang ornaments from the cobwebs draping from your ceiling.
5. The dust balls under your bed have calcified and are large enough to use as bowling balls.
6. There's been a No Vacancy sign on your roach motel for the past three months.

Martha Bolton

DAY
154

"God gave my parents lots of patience.
I wish I hadn't used up so much of it."

Beverly Laudie

DAY 155

SOMETIMES
I THINK
I might have
ATTENTION
DEFICIT... oh look!
A Blue Jay!!!
KS

DAY
156

Seen on a Bumper Sticker

God loves you a latte.

DAY
157

On Heaven . . .

"My dad will be the angel in heaven who knows how to operate a miter saw."

John Peterson

DAY
158

"No water's too deep
with God as your floaties."

Amy Trowbridge-Yates

DAY 159

TV or Not TV: A Christian Television Commercial We Hope We Never See

"Hi, I'm Ben-Hur. You know, those full-contact chariot races can be hard on the old bod. That's why Ben-Hur uses Ben-Gay. It soothes my aching muscles and makes me feel warm and tingly all over. It truly is the balm of balms!"

DAY
160

Bulletin Bloopers

The eighth-graders will be presenting Shakespeare's Hamlet in the church basement Friday at 7 p.m. The entire congregation is invited to attend this tragedy.

Next Sunday afternoon, Farmer Jones will host our youth, giving them a behind-the-scenes tour of his diary.

Our Low-Self-Esteem Support Group will meet Thursday at 6:30 p.m. (Please enter through the back door.)

The pastor would appreciate it if the ladies of the congregation would lend him their electric girdles for the pancake breakfast next Sunday morning.

The Ladies' Bible Study will be held Thursday morning at 10. Lunch will be served in the Fellowship Hall after the Ladies are done with the B.S.

DAY 161

I can do all things–
through prayer and coffee!

DAY 162

ONE DAY IT HAPPENS.

You think to yourself,
"You know, that music
is kind of loud,"
and you reach over
and turn it down.

DAY
164

"What the world really needs is more love and less paperwork."

Pearl Bailey

DAY
165

Bulletin Bloopers

Please continue to pray for Mrs. Witherspoon
and everyone who has to deal with her.

No dunking on the basketball court at St. Theresa's.
If you can think of a way to sprinkle,
go for it.

Softball game against Our Lady of Prophecy next
Thursday will be cancelled due to rain. Trust us.

Don't forget our annual Bargain Basement Fund-
Raiser, to be held in the Upper Hall next Sunday.

Signs from God

GOD WANTS
SPIRITUAL FRUIT,
NOT RELIGIOUS
NUTS.

DAY 167

Ask the Theological Know-How Dudes

Q: On the subject of politics, do you support term limits for Congress?

A: We do not support such limits. We believe congresspersons should have to serve their full prison terms, just like all the other criminals.

DAY 168

Abdication: Giving up on ever having ripped abs.

Incarnation: How a bee often describes its whereabouts.

Airborne: When a woman gives birth on a 747.

Diversification: Skipping the last verse of a song.

Politics: Ticks that attack only politicians.

The Ten Commandments for Mothers

Thou shalt drive the car pool to the ends of the earth.

Thou shalt find the missing sock.

Thou shalt cut both pieces of cake EXACTLY the same size.

Thou shalt NOT get sick when the kids do.

Thou shalt answer questions about geography, long division, and where babies come from.

Thou shalt walk slowly and carry a big purse.

Thou shalt stop on the highway to rescue the turtle . . . and give the kids raw hot dogs to feed it.

Thou shalt smile through a zillion recitals and ball games.

Thou shalt not admit thou art related to—much less kiss— thine adolescent in public.

Thou shalt give thyself time to relax and enjoy life.

Ginnie Job

Bulletin Bloopers

The choir will be practicing every Wednesday—until they get it right.

A reminder: Prayer requests will be taken until we can take no more.

Fasting Group meets for breakfast Saturdays at Pancake Plaza.

We want your clothes for the Clothing Drive, and for Work Day, we want your body.

Top Five Rejected Songs to
Accompany the Offering

"We're in the Money"
"Diamonds Are a Girl's Best Friend"
"Brother, Can You Spare a Dime?"
"Theme from Goldfinger"
"She Works Hard for the Money"

DAY
174

Moldy Oldies

Remember shows like Wagon Train?
Nehi soda? Dick and Jane?
Twelve-inch black-and-white TVs?
Shiny metal Christmas trees?
Groovy songs The Monkees sang?
Astronauts who peddled Tang?
Beehive hair-dos? Monster flicks?
Shake-a-Pudd'n? Space Food Sticks?
Words like "spiffy," "boss," and "keen?"
Super-leaded gasoline?
Hand-pushed mowers for the lawn?
Thank God those good-old days are gone!

Scott Emmons

Bulletin Bloopers

Don't miss next week's Chili Supper,
the perfect way to un-wind!

Men's Basketball this Tuesday. Watch as we give Our
Lady of Sorrows something to cry about.

The recycling fund-raiser encourages you to haul
your cans to church, whether they are big or small.

Remember in prayer the many who are sick of
our community.

A Note on Church Music

Bell choirs are a great idea for people who want to contribute to worship in some way that doesn't require playing a complicated instrument or singing. And it helps if they look good in gloves, but it's not a deal-breaker.

Another advantage: The tension level is some-what lower in bell choirs than in other choirs, and way lower than in "praise bands." Also, fewer ego problems.

DAY
178

A Holiday Observation

If your Christmas Eve service doesn't involve candles being held by some people who really shouldn't handle fire, you're missing one of the most exciting elements of the holy season.

DAY
179

Sunday Sartorial Splendor

Growing up, you had school shoes, play shoes, and church shoes, and there was no mixing. You could not go to school in play shoes. You could not worship in school shoes.

Including travel time, you wore those church shoes maybe three hours a week. Which is about how long you spent looking for them every Sunday morning. Where did they go between Sunday afternoon and Saturday night? And if you did find one shoe, there was no guarantee that the other was nearby.

If you were a boy, you had church pants. These could not be jeans. They could be corduroy, but only if you disliked corduroy. They could not button or snap—they had to close with that metal tab that slid under the tiny metal bridge. During the week, that bridge would collapse, so the tab would never fit. Your mom had to pry it open with a butter knife. Then you had to add a belt, which took time to find, as it had apparently run off with the missing shoe.

DAY
180

How Great Thou "Art"

Nice moms let kids draw on the bulletin during "big people's" church. Mean moms make the kid sit still with hands in lap, watching wistfully the kids with nice moms draw, make airplanes, maybe even play tic-tac-toe with a brother or sister.

No mom, however, lets any kid play that paper football game during church; that's over the line. Also, for reasons they cannot explain, most moms seem to be uncomfortable about permitting origami.

DAY
181

"Always do right. This will gratify some people and astonish the rest."

Mark Twain

DAY
182

Seen on a Bumper Sticker

Whatever your lot in life,
build something on it!

SPOT THE DIFFERENCE:

CRAZY PERSON

HANDS-FREE CELL PHONE USER

DAY 184

A stitch in time saves nine . . . but a stapler's a whole lot faster!

Scratch my back, and I'll scratch yours. But next time, let's stay out of the poison ivy.

Paddle your own canoe—but take it out of the bathtub when you're done.

Opportunity knocks but once. It's the door-to-door salesman who'll keep on knocking and ringing until you answer.

Look before you leap; someone might have drained the pool!

Martha Bolton

DAY
185

A Potluck Tip

Bring a bucket of chicken to one potluck, and
nobody will think anything of it. Two times—a few
people notice. On that third bucket in a row, don't be
surprised to find yourself on a prayer list somewhere.
Probably under a generic heading like "unspoken
need" or "issues."

DAY
186

God's "Judgment"

Maybe "judgmental" is spelled without the "e" after "judge" so that most of us will spell it wrong at least once and perhaps be a little less critical of others, knowing that we, too, are flawed.

DAY
187

Good Sportsmanship

Church softball games, especially those pitting really good teams against one another, are a much better indicator of who swears and who doesn't than one's behavior at church on Sunday mornings. An even better indicator would be the Men's Group Golf Scramble.

DAY
188

A Modest Proposal

Churches where they let you bring coffee into the
sanctuary—or even more so if they actually serve
coffee—should never, ever have a service that lasts
more than an hour. And that's pushing it.

DAY
189

Sympathy for the Apostles' Kids

Growing up as a child of one of the Apostles must have been tough. Like being a preacher's kid times a thousand. And without the Internet to blog about your feelings? Brutal.

DAY
190

If you're Happy
and you kNow it
cLamp YOUR HaMs!

DAY
191

Did the biblical prophets get tired of friends
constantly asking if the weekend weather would be
nice for a picnic?

DAY
193

If you go to a church that has volunteer cleaners and you're one of them, good for you! You probably work very hard at a mostly thankless job. But consider this: People at church are obliged to forgive you, even if you do a slacker job of the cleaning. Takes some of the pressure off, doesn't it?

DAY
194

Church choir robes make everyone look the same.
But is "bad" a good thing to have in common?

Say something nice to your pastor's wife. She has
a hard job for which she is not paid.

DAY
196

You've Been Warned

"My church's Youth Minister is hipper than your church's Youth Minister!" is not a fight anyone can win.

DAY 197

THE BAD NEWS:

YOUR VISION GETS WORSE AS YOU GET OLDER.

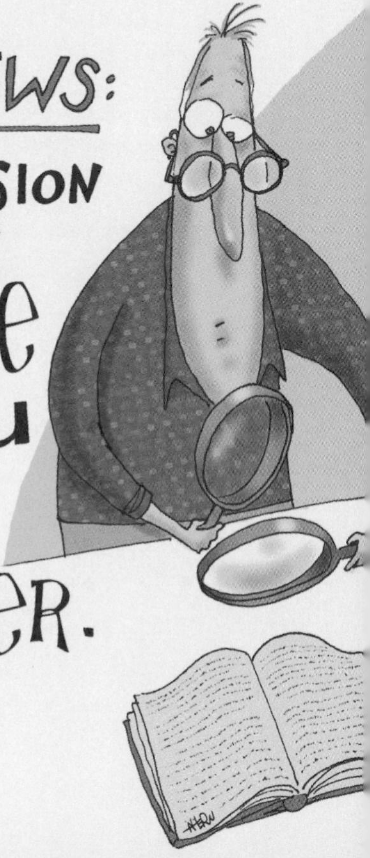

DAY
198

Falling asleep during your church's "quiet time" is
not the biggest sin in the universe. The disciples did
it, for example. And they had Jesus around. So don't
beat yourself up about nodding off once in a while;
you're in good company.

DAY
199

Shouldn't the past-tense of "preach" be "praught?"
Try using it; see if you can get it to catch on.

DAY
201

If you volunteer to help lead the junior-high camping
and canoe trip—even though you are not a parent to
a junior-higher—and you capsize, smack your head
on a rock, and drown, you go straight to Heaven.
Also, you get to bring one pet of your choice (but no
ferrets, please).

DAY
202

Was Mary's sister Martha bitter because she got stuck with the old-lady name?

DAY
203

Why aren't more people—or any people—
named Lazarus these days?

DAY
204

DAY
205

A Modest Proposal

On the one Sunday a year that the "youth" are in charge of the service, everyone sings fun songs and pays better attention to the sermon. Maybe two Youth Sundays a year would be a good idea?

DAY 207

No matter how good the praise and worship band at your church may be, do not, under any circumstances, give them that "rock and roll" salute, the one with the extended pinkie and index finger. People will freak out. And not in a good way.

DAY
208

When the disciples went out to eat, would they
always insist on a table for twelve, or did they
sometimes have to split up into two groups of six,
or possibly three groups of four?

DAY
209

Fun Things to Say at Church Potlucks

"Is there a vegan meal available?"

"What, exactly, are the rules about gluttony?"

"So, I guess 'drinking the Kool Aid' is OK now?"

"Is it cool for me to designate who I'd like to be
Heimliched by, just in case?"

It's the latest thing. It's called the veterinarian diet.

DAY
212

Seen on a Bumper Sticker

How's my walk with God?
Call 1-800-CHURCH ME

DAY
213

A Halloween Tip

If your church does that "alternative" Halloween thing, in which kids are supposed to dress as Bible characters, it really opens the options up if you suggest that there were probably pirates in Bible times.

DAY
214

Are the streets of heaven still made of gold if we're no longer on the gold standard?

DAY
215

A Church Fashion Tip

If you wear business casual clothing to church
nowadays, that's OK. But if you are wearing golf
clothes, well, eyebrows will be raised.

DAY
216

You've Been Warned

You might be surprised, upon finishing reading the
entire Bible in a Year®™, that there is no prize for
reading the entire Bible in a year.

DAY 217

On falling asleep in church: Sitting very still in a place where it's pretty quiet, except for some soothing organ music, is not the best way to avoid napping.

Clean living paid off,
and Leslie ended up going to Heaven.

DAY
220

Q: Please settle a Sunday school argument: was Zaccheus the shortest man in the Bible?

A: Nope, Little Zack was actually third-shortest. You're forgetting Knee-High-Emiah, a truly minor prophet, and the New Testament Roman centurion— the one who fell asleep on his watch. You can't get much smaller than that.

DAY 221

If the Hebrew language has no vowels, does it only sometimes not have 'y'?

Crunching Numbers, Bible Style

Is there something inherently evil about page 666
in a Bible? Shouldn't it just be skipped, like the 13th
floor in hotels? What if you were in a hotel that did
have a floor 13, and you opened the Gideon Bible to
page 666! What then?

DAY
223

Every few years, someone says he's found Noah's Ark. Why is it always Noah's Ark? How about Goliath's sandals or Lot's wife or something?

DAY
226

When we were kids, why were the least comfortable, least flattering, least favorite clothes we owned our "church clothes?"

The Still, Small Voice

Ever walked around in an empty church at night?
Kind of scary. Especially the auditorium part.
Mostly because you think maybe you're going to
get asked to go do something really hard. As a rule,
God asked people to do hard things when they
wandered alone in a house of worship. No one
ever heard a voice saying, "Thou shalt go hang out
at the mall. Maybe have a Cinnabon."

DAY
228

Much Sunday school and Children's Church time is devoted to memorizing the names of the tribes of Israel. But how many of life's big problems have been solved by memorizing the names of the tribes of Israel?

DAY
230

A Tip for the Christmas Season

This time around, be sensitive to guys growing
beards for Passion Plays. Not everyone goes all
Grizzly Adams overnight.

DAY
231

Gambling is regarded as a sin. Church raffles
and Bingo are OK. Discuss.

Signs from God

LOCKMAN COMMUNITY CHURCH

TOLERANCE IN ALL THINGS.

(EXCEPT FOR THE ONES
WE'VE TALKED ABOUT.)

DAY
234

Bang the Drum Holy

It's been maybe 30 years since drums showed up in lots of church worship bands, but drummers still look nervous and jittery in front of a congregation— like they think someone's going to come along and say, "Drums! We can't have drums in church!" And the jig will be up. On the other hand, all drummers just naturally look nervous and jittery, so maybe that's it.

DAY
235

Which was more disillusioning: learning there was no Santa Claus, or discovering that "cleanliness is next to godliness" is NOT, in fact, in the Bible?

DAY
237

Bunko Night!

See church ladies rolling dice,
sipping fizzy drinks on ice,
munching cookies, cakes, and more.
Anybody keeping score?
Just this morning, Joan was stressed.
Jan was moody, Val depressed.
Everyone was in a funk-o
till they had their night of Bunko!

While they're playing, hear them chat.
Paula's niece is such a brat!
Carla plans to take a cruise.
Lynn just bought the cutest shoes!
Cheryl's got a brand-new hubby
(handsome, though he's sorta chubby).
Cindy's boyfriend's quite a hunk-o.
Gotta dish while playing Bunko.
Bunko! Bunko! Quite a hunk-o.
Gossip goes so well with Bunko!

Scott Emmons

DAY
238

Did Jesus' disciple Thaddeus resent not having as
normal a name as Matthew or Peter or John?

The "Missing Glasses"
Support Group

DAY
240

A Worship Service Tip

Try not to discern the voices of individual singers in
congregational settings. Most of the singers you'd
want to single out are up front, in the choir.

DAY
241

Why do people call a circumstance "God's Timing" only when they don't get what they want?

DAY
242

Signs from God

HARRISONVILLE CHURCH

WE'RE LOOKING
FOR A FEW
GOOD SINNERS.

DAY
243

How did Welch's get to be the grape juice?
Do the Welches know somebody?

DAY
244

Signs from God

Sandalwood Baptist Church

THE PERFECT CHURCH
FOR PEOPLE WHO AREN'T
EVEN CLOSE TO PERFECT.

DAY
245

Top Ten Least Popular Bible Names

10. Ananias

 9. Sapphira

 8. Pontius

 7. Kevin

 6. Methuselah

 5. Jehoshaphat

 4. Jezebel

 3. Bathsheba

 2. Mephibosheth

 1. Judas

Other options: Whore of Babylon (more of a nickname), Herod, James the Lesser, Tricia

DAY 246

BEFORE RUSHING into A FACE-LIFT,
Kim CHECKS OUT HOW it LOOKS
On the CAT.

DAY
247

Bulletin Bloopers

A reminder during tax time: don't let worry kill you—let the church help.

Your assignment for this week: Smile at someone who is hard to love. Say "hell!" to a total stranger you meet on the street.

Just a reminder: The lavatory on the upper level is broken; please go in the basement.

The size-two choir robe is in. Next week's sermon: Dealing with Jealousy.

DAY
248

Signs from God

ST. JOSEPH'S of Malden

WELCOME TO
OUR CHURCH!
(SKATEBOARDERS WILL BE PROSECUTED.)

DAY
249

Does something bad happen to you if you throw out
an old Bible?

DAY
250

Church Bingo

Maturing's a pleasure!
It's all that you could wish.
That zesty nonfat yogurt dip
is heaven in a dish!
Oh, the thrill of church-night Bingo!
Staying up till half past eight!
Doing 35 or 40
on a busy interstate!
That elevator music really makes us tap our toes,
and there's nothing more exciting than comparing
HMOs!
There's heavy-duty denture grip
to keep us always grinning.
So now's the time to celebrate
'cause life is just beginning!

Scott Emmons

Something to Ponder

Is it shallow to pray that somebody will bring the really good peach pie to a potluck supper?

OFFICE PARTIES IN HELL

DAY
254

Signs from God

Beaumont Community Church

IF YOU'RE GOING
TO SLEEP SOMEWHERE
SUNDAY MORNING,
MIGHT AS WELL BE HERE.

DAY 255

Bulletin Bloopers

Eight new choir robes are currently needed, due to the addition of several new members and the deterioration of some older ones.

At the evening service tonight, the sermon topic will be "What Is Hell?" Come early and listen to our choir practice.

A bean supper will be held on Tuesday evening in the church hall. Music will follow.

Irving Benson and Jessie Carter were married on October 24 in the church. So ends a friendship that began in their school days.

This being Easter Sunday, we will ask Mrs. Lewis to come forward before the service and lay an egg on the altar.

DAY
256

Are Mondays really "days that the Lord hath made?"
And if so, why hath He?

DAY
257

Little-Known Old Testament Facts

The chunks of the Wall of Jericho autographed by Joshua and available on eBay are not authentic.

A big part of what made Queen Vashti so attractive in the first place was very flattering lighting.

Moses did not look all that much like Charlton Heston. He looked more like James Garner near the end of The Rockford Files.

Signs from God

Westwood Congregational Church

AIR CONDITIONED!
(WHICH IS MORE THAN
WE CAN SAY FOR HELL.)

DAY
259

Things I Would Change, If I Could

Ice cream would not cause brain freezes;
infomercials would.

Dusting, not chocolate, would cause acne.

Work week = two days. Weekends = five days.

The calories would be removed from banana splits
and put into Brussels sprouts.

Naps would burn as many calories as marathons.

Martha Bolton

DAY
260

Signs from God

DAY
261

Bulletin Bloopers

Memorial Offering: Please place your donation in the envelope, along with the deceased person(s) you want remembered.

For those of you who have children and don't know it, we have a nursery downstairs.

Our Boy Scouts are saving aluminum cans, bottles, and other items to be recycled. Proceeds will be used to cripple children.

The senior choir invites any member of the congregation who enjoys sinning to join us right away!

DAY
262

Wouldn't It Be Great

Wouldn't it be great if we could have FBI technology
at our disposal when deciding whom to marry?
We could scan their pictures into those nifty FBI
computers, then have them virtually aged to see
exactly what we are saying "I do" to.

Anita Renfroe

DAY
263

Signs from God

IF YOU CAN
READ THIS,
THANK GOD.

Little-Known New Testament Facts

Some of the people who look like they're taking notes during sermons are secretly seeing how many words can be made from the letters in "Corinthians."

Nearly 17% of the people who heard the original Sermon on the Mount thought it "ran a little long."

Had it been invented—and had they found the time—the remaining 11 apostles would have made a fine football team.

DAY 266

Martha's Kitchen Tips

A calendar should never be used as a timer.

Carving your turkey should not require a two-man lumberjack saw.

Do not confuse moldy cheese with your chia pet!

A potato may have eyes, but discard your potato salad immediately if it winks at you.

A meat loaf should never be used for dinner mood-lighting – no matter how brightly it is glowing.

Martha Bolton

DAY 267

↑

Ignored her mother's advice.

DAY 268

Bulletin Bloopers

Middle schoolers meet every Sunday in the basement. You have been warned.

The Middle School Youth Group trip to the Alligator Farm has been cancelled due to an outbreak of common sense.

Bring a side dish to the potluck lunch next Sunday. Don't ask questions; just bring a side dish.

Reminder: Prayer requests are confidential, seen only by the members of the Prayer Group. (Please join our Prayer Group, meeting Wednesdays. Everyone's invited!)

DAY
269

Signs from God

Koinonia CHurcH

50% LESS JUDGMENTAL
THAN EVERYONE ELSE.

DAY
270

Potluck supper Sunday at 5. Prayer and medication to follow.

Don't forget; on New Year's Eve the church will host an evening of fine dining, superb entertainment, and gracious hostility.

Attend our prayer breakfast next Saturday! You will hear an excellent speaker and heave a hearty meal!

Yet another Youth Group bonfire has been cancelled. (We really might not plan any more Youth Group bonfires.)

DAY 271

Flippant: An ant who's a gymnast.

Gastrointestinal: The stomach ache you get after paying the high price of gasoline.

Cauliflower: Lassie's corsage.

Homage: The age of your house.

Category: A horror flick about cats.

DAY 272

Seen on a Bumper Sticker

If 10% of my income is good enough for God, why isn't it good enough for the IRS?

DAY
273

Today's Quote

"I was thinking about how people seem to read the Bible a lot more as they get older, then it dawned on me: they're cramming for their final exam."

George Carlin

DAY 275

A Beatitude by George

"Blessed is the man who, having nothing to say, abstains from giving wordy evidence of the fact."

George Eliot

DAY
276

Opportunity knocks once;
temptation bangs on your door forever.

DAY 277

People are funny; they want the front of the bus, the middle of the road, and the back of the church.

DAY
279

"The English are not very spiritual people, so they invented cricket to give them some idea of eternity."

George Bernard Shaw

DAY
280

Seen on a Bumper Sticker

Jesus loves the hell out of you!

DAY
282

Signs from God

First Baptist Church

**STANDING ON
THE PROMISES**
(NOT JUST SITTING
ON THE PREMISES)

DAY
283

Coincidence: When God chooses
to remain anonymous.

DAY
285

"To err is human; to blame the error on somebody else is even more human."

John Nadeau

Signs from God

DAY
287

"Stacy, does your family say a prayer before
each meal?"
"No, we don't have to; my mom's a good cook!"

"HE HAD 13 ITEMS."

DAY
290

"The good Lord didn't create anything without a purpose, but the fly comes close."

Mark Twain

DAY
291

Why didn't Noah just swat his two mosquitoes?

DAY
292

Seen on a Bumper Sticker

Prayer is like wireless access to God—
with no roaming fees.

DAY
293

"To be clever enough to get all the money,
one must be stupid enough to want it."

G.K. Chesterton

JIM PAYS THE PRICE FOR WRITING AN
EXTREMELY PERSONAL CHECK.

DAY
296

Bulletin Bloopers

This afternoon there will be congregational meetings in the South and North ends of the church. Children will be baptized at both ends.

At the conclusion of today's service, a special collection will be taken to defray the cost of the new carpet. All those wishing to do something on the carpet should come forward and do so.

Our special music this morning will be provided by Dale Anderson, DDS. He will be singing "Crown Him with Many Crowns."

DAY
297

Signs from God

DAY
298

The All-Church Football Team

Art Monk

Ricky Churchman

Ray Sermon

Frank Pope

Freddie Joe Nunn

Lemar Parrish

Richard Bishop

Randy Cross

Jerome Heavens

Dave Chapple

Paul Blessings

DAY
299

Signs from God

CHURCH of CHRIST

WE'RE LIKE FUDGE—
REALLY SWEET WITH
A FEW NUTS.

DAY 300

Bulletin Bloopers

Please note: While our pastor is on vacation, massages can be given to the church secretary.

Last Sunday's worship concert was a huge success. Special thanks to Jennifer, the pastor's daughter, who volunteered to play piano, which fell on her, as usual.

Thanks to our missionaries to Mexico who spoke very briefly last week—much to the delight of the audience.

Terry Jones will play this Sunday's offertory, "Jesus Paid It All."

Due to the Rector's illness, Wednesday's healing service will be postponed until further notice.

DAY
301

Seen on a Bumper Sticker

Don't give the Devil an inch;
he'll become your ruler.

DAY
303

Bulletin Bloopers

A reminder: Once the service has begun, please wait in the vestibule. Ushers will eat all late-comers.

This morning, Miss Charlene will sing "I Shall Not Pass This Way Again," and surely bring delight to everyone in attendance.

Service note: the third verse of "Blessed Assurance" will be sung without any musical accomplishment.

Please join us in prayer for Allen and Amy as they prepare for the girth of their first child.

This week's songfest will be hell at United Methodist Church.

DAY 304

The Christian and the Lion

One day in ancient Rome, a lion chased a Christian through the streets. Finally, it became obvious to the exhausted man that the lion was going to catch him. So he turned suddenly, dropped to his knees, and prayed, "Lord, please make this lion a Christian!"

Instantly, the lion dropped to his knees too. He folded his forepaws in front of his face and prayed, "Dear Lord, for this meal of which I am about to partake . . ."

DAY
305

"The secret of a good sermon is to have a good beginning and a good ending, then having the two as close together as possible."

George Burns

Adam and Eve disobeyed God by eating one bad apple,
so they were driven from the Garden of Eden.
(Not sure what they were driven in, because there were no cars.)

Adam and Eve had a son, Cain, who hated his
brother as long as he was Abel.

One of the next important people was Noah, who
built a large boat and put his family— including his
wife, Joan of Ark—and some animals on it.

Then there was Moses, who led the Israel Lights
out of Egypt and away from the evil Pharaoh after
God sent ten plagues on Pharaoh's people. The plagues
included frogs, mice, lice, bowels, and no cable TV.

After God helped the Israel Lights escape, He fed
them every day with manicotti from heaven. Then
He gave them His Top Ten Commandments. These
include: Don't lie, cheat, smoke, dance, or covet your
neighbor's bottom.

DAY 307

The New Testament appears in the Bible, right after the Old one. The New Testament is 2,000 years old, so why is it called "new?"

Jesus is the star of the New Testament. He was born in Bethlehem, in a barn. Also, Jesus was born on Christmas day, so I feel kinda sorry for Him, having His birthday so close to Christmas and all.

Jesus had 12 opossums. The worst one was Judas Asparagus. Judas was so evil that they named a terrible vegetable after him.

Jesus was a great man. He healed many leopards. But then the Republicans put Jesus on trial before Pontius, the Pilot. Pilot should have stuck up for Jesus, but he just washed his hands instead.

Jesus died for our sins, then came back to life again. He went up to Heaven. His return is foretold in the book of Revolution.

DAY 310

Getting the Pastor's Goat

A young couple invited their aging pastor to their home for dinner one Sunday. While the couple was in the kitchen, preparing to serve the meal, the pastor leaned toward the couple's five-year-old son. "What are we having to eat?" he asked.

"Goat!" the boy replied.

The pastor frowned at the boy. "Goat?" he said. "Really?"

"Oh, yes," the boy nodded. "They've been talking about it all week—having the old goat for Sunday dinner!"

DAY
311

Words of Gold?

A minister's car broke down on his way home from Sunday service. He walked home, then called his town's only mechanic on Monday morning. The mechanic met the pastor where the stalled car sat and began his repairs.

"I'm going to go easy with you on the cost, Reverend," the mechanic said after several minutes.

"Thank you so much," the man of the cloth replied. "After all, I'm just a poor preacher."

"I know," the mechanic said. "I heard your sermon yesterday."

DAY
312

A Pastor's Proverb

"Doubts are the ants in the pants of faith.
They keep it awake and moving."

Frederick Buechner

DAY
313

Why do the Pentecostal church parking lots
have handicap spaces?

DAY
314

"Sometimes I lie awake at night and I ask, 'Where I
have I gone wrong?' Then a voice says to me, 'This is
going to take more than one night.'"

Charlie Brown

DAY
315

A Preacher's Proverb

"The length of a sermon should be directly related
to the capacity of the average human bladder."

The Rev. Jerry Springston

DAY 316

Tracey begins to wonder if she's supporting too many causes.

DAY
317

Top Five Church Pickup Lines

1. "Hey, baby, what's your spiritual gift?"

2. "No, this pew isn't saved, but I sure am!"

3. "This sermon's dull—wanna try to start 'The Wave?'"

4. "Do you know I can bench-press an entire set of Bible commentaries?"

5. "Do you have a brother named Gabriel? Because I'm sure you're an angel!"

DAY
318

"Gray hair is God's graffiti."

Bill Cosby

DAY
319

Don't let the car fool you;
my treasures are in heaven.

A Fishy Excuse

Saint Peter halted a man at the entrance to heaven.

"I'm sorry," the saint told the man, "but I cannot admit you. You've told too many lies."

"C'mon, Pete, give me a break," the man pleaded. "After all, you were once a fisherman yourself!"

One Day in the First Baptist Church Office . . .

Church Secretary Janet: "Pastor, there is a problem with your BlackBerry; there's moisture in the circuitry."

Pastor Bob: "Moisture in the circuitry? That doesn't make any sense. The air in here is as dry as a desert."

Church Secretary Janet: "I'm telling you, sir, that there is moisture in the circuitry."

Pastor Bob: "That's ridiculous. You're not a techie. You don't even know what circuitry is. Where is my BlackBerry anyway?"

Church Secretary Janet: "At the bottom of the baptistery."

DAY
324

"The trouble with eating Italian food at pot luck
is that, five or six days later, you're hungry again."

George House

DAY
325

Signs from God

GOD IS WAY
TOO BIG TO
FIT IN ONE
DENOMINATION.

Today's Quote

"Anyone who thinks we don't do burnt offerings anymore has never been to First Baptist of Raymore's Back to Bible School Potluck Dinner."

Dan Taylor

DAY
327

If you can sing the Doxology every single Sunday morning and actually be praising God "from whom all blessings flow," instead of thinking about lunch, you should be preaching sermons or writing books.

Sunday Sleep Guilt

Sleeping in on Sunday morning is not easy when you are intermittently wakened by guilt, after which you fall asleep and then have guilt-induced dreams. When it's finally time for football, you can't even enjoy the pre-game NFL shows because you feel like the sportscasters, with their smug smiles, are judging you.

DAY
329

The Parable of the Prodigal Son

Feeling footloose, a fellow forced his fawning father to fork over a fraction of the family farthings. Then the fop fled to foreign fields, where he frittered his fortune, feasting among fair-weather friends until he found himself a feed-flinger in a filthy farmyard.

Flummoxed, the fugitive found his faculties and returned to his father. "Father!" he fumbled. "I've failed and forfeited favor! Even a flunkie would fare better!"

"Folks, the fugitive is found!" the father flailed," Let fanfares flare!"

Unfortunately, older brother Frank was unforgiving. "Father!" he fumed. "Forsooth. That fool forfeited his fortune!"

"Frank," the father confronted. "Don't fester. Your coffers are filled. But your phantom brother is finally back in the fold."

Thus, a fugitive found fulfillment. Further, the father's forgiveness formed the foundation for a fugitive's future. For a faithful father loves forever.

Signs from God

BETHANY BAPTIST CHURCH

IF YOU ATTENDED HERE,
YOU'D BE HOLY NOW.

DAY
332

The Bald Truth

Pastor Mortimer Clay bought a tacky toupee.
A tacky toupee that he wears every day.
It's curly and red, rather big for his head,
and it sits just a little askew.
Mortimer preens like a kid in his teens,
a kid in his teens wearing low-rider jeans.
His 10-dollar rug makes him cocky and smug.
What he ought to have bought was a clue!

Scott Emmons

DAY
333

Signs from God

COME WORK FOR
THE LORD. THE WORK
IS HARD; THE PAY
IS LOW. BUT THE
RETIREMENT BENEFITS
ARE OUT OF
THIS WORLD.

DAY 334

"A good sermon should be like a woman's skirt
—short enough to arouse interest but long enough
to cover the essentials."

Ronald Knox

DAY
335

"Greater love hath no man than this: to attend the Episcopal church with his wife."

President Lyndon B. Johnson

DAY
336

Leftover Rules

Are your leftovers worthy of bringing to the next
church potluck? Follow these guidelines.

1. Carefully unwrap or uncover the item in question,
then sniff like a curious canine. Does the aroma
match the item in question? (If this exercise makes
you cry, do not bring this item to church under any
circumstances. Don't even put it in your compost
heap. After all, maggots have feelings too.)

2. Study the food for mold. If it has grown more
hair than Esau, ironically, it's not fit for church.

3. The serve-ability of packaged foods is easy to
determine. Just check the expiration date. If Richard
M. Nixon was still in office, beware. After all, look
where Richard M. Nixon is today.

DAY
338

Something to Ponder

Why are church people so kind, polite, and
sweet-spirited—until you try to sit in their pew?

A Day in the Life of Adam

Can you imagine Adam sneaking up behind Eve and putting his hands over her eyes . . .

"Guess who?"

"Adam, you are so silly!"

"Ah, you guessed right again, Eve. You're pretty smart for someone made from a rib."

"Whatever, Adam. Let's go down by the peach tree and have some dinner."

"Ooh, I love peaches. You know me so well. There's just no other woman in the world for me!"

"You can say that again!"

"Hey, Eve, after dinner, let's go for a romantic walk to the center of the garden."

"I don't know, sweetie. That serpent likes to hang out down there. And he creeps me out."

"Ah, relax, baby. What harm can a little snake do?"

DAY
340

Theological positions that are set in stone are heavy—and that's about all they have going for them.

DAY
341

My Motto, by Jan Barett

Veni, vidi, Visa.

(We came, we saw, we went shopping.)

DAY 342

TV or Not TV: Christian Television Commercials We Hope We Never See

"Hello, I'm Noah. I'm here to talk to you about irregularity. As you probably know, irregularity is no fun. It's worse than being cooped up with an ark full of smelly animals. That's why, if you're feeling a bit bound up, I urge you to try my new Noah's Laxative! Just look for the box with the big rainbow on it. Then take the tablets two by two, and you'll receive up to 40 days of gentle, effective relief. That's a promise. Just make sure that when the flood eventually hits, you're in the right place!"

DAY
343

"When you reach your wit's end,
you'll find God waiting there for you."

The Rev. Robert St. John

Are You a True Baptist?

If you're wondering, take the following self-test.

1. The closest I get to dancing is trying to wriggle into my girdle before Easter Service. (Women only on this one, please.)

2. I think Andy Williams is OK, but I wish he'd slow the tempo!

3. I believe pew cushions are for wimps.

4. For me, "wine" in the Bible is properly translated "Welch's 100% Grape Juice."

5. I think Beethoven was OK, but that Fanny Crosby—there's a real musical genius!

6. My creed: A sermon that ends before noon, ain't a real sermon!

7. I discard my swimming suit when it gets a hole in the knee.

8. My idea of a rock group? Mount Rushmore.

If you answered yes to seven or more questions, you are a Baptist in good standing. In fact, Pat Robertson would probably like to have you over for dinner. But please call first.

DAY
346

If a pastor questions his wife's judgment when he's in the forest, with no one around to hear him, is he still wrong?

DAY
347

Q: I just started college and don't know which major to choose. Your advice?

A: We recommend that you major in Communications, just like your beloved Theological Know-How Dudes. That way, when you ask "Paper or plastic?" you'll really be able to get your message across!

DAY
349

Clean Jean

Jean's a model citizen.
She follows every rule.
She never ran a yellow light
or cut a class in school.
But even Jean, whose nose is clean,
is often heard to say,
"I'd break the law of gravity
if I could find a way!"

Scott Emmons

DAY
350

A Modest Proposal

If your church ever prays for anything besides health issues and travel, you are at an advanced level. Something like 87% of all audible church prayers are requested for one of these two categories. But, this being the case, shouldn't there be more prayers for safe travel to a hospital?

ARE TANGERINES REALLY JUST ORANGES THAT DiDN'T WANT iT ENOUGH?

DAY
352

Knowing the Drill

An observation about those "Sword Drills" so many
churches employ: Many children are surprised
to find that as they face grown-up challenges and
problems, the ability to find verses in the Bible really-
very-super-fast is not that helpful.

Something to Ponder

Why is alcohol rarely, if ever, served at any kind
of church function? This is ironic, since church
functions so often make people feel like drinking.

DAY
354

Little-Known Theological Fact

You can win pretty much any theological argument by being the first one to say that God told you whatever it is your point may be.

For example: "Should we go to McDonald's or Taco Bell?"

Try this tactic and you'll be enjoying Nachos Bell Grande while your theologically impaired opponent bitterly fantasizes about a Big Mac.

DAY
355

Signs from God

PLAN AHEAD.
REMEMBER, IT WASN'T
RAINING WHEN
NOAH BUILT THE ARK.

DAY
356

Why do the differences between Conferences,
Synods, Branches, and Sects matter only to the
people in those Conferences, Synods, Branches,
and Sects?

DAY
357

Bulletin Bloopers

Don't miss Pastor Ted's moving massage tonight at 6.

The outreach committee needs 25 volunteers to call on people who are not afflicted with any church.

Weight Watchers will meet at 7 p.m. at the First Presbyterian Church. Please enter through the large double doors at the side of the building.

Worship Reminder: The congregation is asked to remain seated until the end of the recession.

DAY
358

HOW PARENTS SEE THEMSELVES.

HOW KIDS SEE THEIR PARENTS!

DAY
359

The Hair of Many Colors

Samantha's hair is chestnut brown.
Last week it was espresso.
The month before? I can't recall.
Light apricot? I guess so.
It's gone from quince to sandalwood
to sunny Santa Fe.
And when Sam's old and much more bold,
she might just try it gray.

Scott Emmons

DAY
360

Signs from God

"Greetings, folks. I'm Jacob."

"And I'm his brother Esau. We're here to tell you about the fantastic new Jacob & Esau coat from Land of Canaan Fog."

"That's right, bro. This coat is reversible—furry on the inside and smooth on the outside. Or maybe it's the other way around . . ."

"That it is, Jake. I like wearing the fur on the outside while I'm in the wild, doing something manly, like hunting. Of course, if you're doing sissy housework, like making soup, I'd go smooth-side out."

"Hey! That was really uncalled for, Esau! I'm taking my reversible coat and leaving."

"This isn't your coat; it's my coat!"

"You're wrong, gorilla boy!"

"Am not, hairless wonder!"

"I'm telling on you, Esau!"

"Daaaaaaaad!"

DAY
362

Sing—loud.

Skip the dishes.

Do cartwheels.

Eat ice cream cones.

Lick up the drips.

Wear your favorite jeans.

Go barefoot.

Make somebody laugh.

Dance in front of the sunset.

Live like the wild and beautiful child of God you are.

Sarah Mueller

DAY
363

Signs from God

DAY 364

Out of the Mouths of Babes

"It's very important to be quiet in church ...
because people are sleeping."

"Jesus, if you can't help me be a good boy, it's OK.
I'm having a good time like I am."

"Grandpa, you are just like God! He's really old, too!"

"Lord, forgive us our trash baskets as we forgive
those who put trash in our baskets."

"And lead us not into temptation, but deliver us from
e-mail. Amen."

DAY
365

And One Final Thought

"I've read the last page of the Bible. It's all going to turn out all right."

The Rev. Billy Graham